Writing Fabulous Sentences & Paragraphs

Grades 1–3

Manufacturer Evan-Moor Corporation
10 Harris Court, Suite C-3 Monterey, CA 93940, USA
www.evan-moor.com

EU Rep. Authorised Rep Compliance Ltd., Ground Floor,
71 Lower Baggot Street, Dublin, D02 P593, Ireland
www.arccompliance.com

Writing: Teera Robinson
Content Editing: Lisa Vitarisi Mathews
Copy Editing: Kathleen Jorgensen
Art Direction: Yuki Meyer
Cover Design: Yuki Meyer
Nathan Jarvis
Illustration: Mary Rojas
Design/Production: Jessica Onken

EVAN-MOOR Educational Publishers

EMC 3135

Visit
teaching-standards.com
to view a correlation
of this book.

Correlated to Current Standards

Congratulations on your purchase of some of the finest teaching materials in the world.

For information about other Evan-Moor products, call 1-800-777-4362, fax 1-800-777-4332, or visit our website, www.evan-moor.com.

10 Harris Court, Suite C-3, Monterey, CA 93940-5773. Printed in China.

CPSIA: Asia Pacific Offset Ltd, Kowloon, Hong Kong, China [6/2025]

002

Contents

What's Inside

Each section of this book includes teaching support pages with suggestions for preparing and delivering the lessons.

Sentences

Pages 10–59 provide instruction and practice with basic sentence structure and writing sentences. Students begin by recognizing sentences, correcting sentences, and adding parts of sentences. They build on these skills by expanding sentences, writing sentences, exercising word choice, and using new vocabulary.

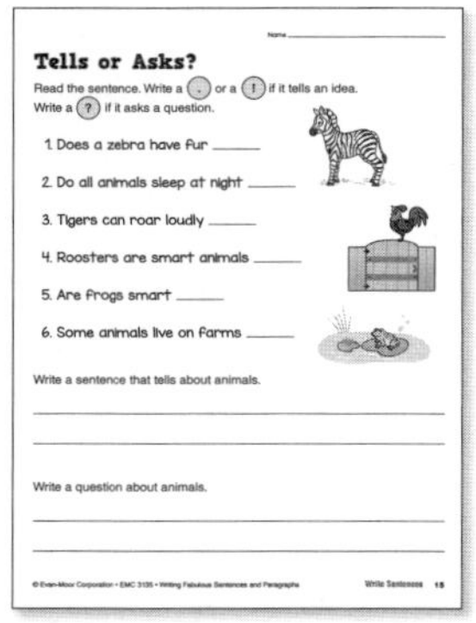

Tells or Asks?

Read the sentence. Write a ⊙ or a ⓘ if it tells an idea.
Write a ⓘ if it asks a question.

1. Does a zebra have fur ____
2. Do all animals sleep at night ____
3. Tigers can roar loudly ____
4. Roosters are smart animals ____
5. Are frogs smart ____
6. Some animals live on farms ____

Write a sentence that tells about animals.

Write a question about animals.

Paragraphs

Pages 60–109 provide instruction and practice in recognizing topic sentences, supporting details, and closing sentences. Students gain valuable practice in writing paragraphs and recognizing different kinds of paragraphs.

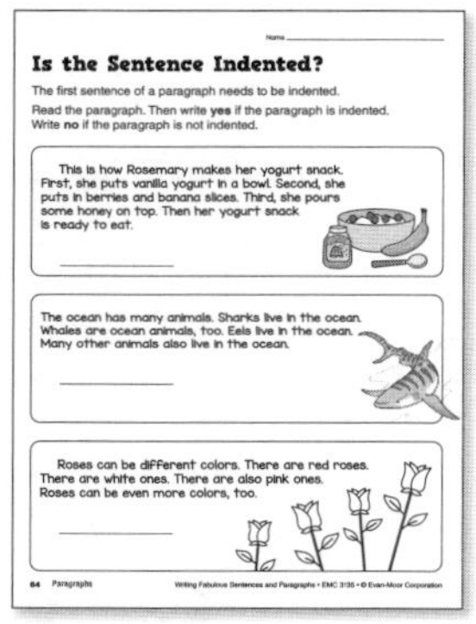

Is the Sentence Indented?

The first sentence of a paragraph needs to be indented.
Read the paragraph. Then write **yes** if the paragraph is indented.
Write **no** if the paragraph is not indented.

This is how Rosemary makes her yogurt snack. First, she puts vanilla yogurt in a bowl. Second, she puts in berries and banana slices. Third, she pours some honey on top. Then her yogurt snack is ready to eat.

The ocean has many animals. Sharks live in the ocean. Whales are ocean animals, too. Eels live in the ocean. Many other animals also live in the ocean.

Roses can be different colors. There are red roses. There are white ones. There are also pink ones. Roses can be even more colors, too.

Concept Charts

Pages 12, 20, 36, 46, 50, 62, 66, and 90 are concept charts for students. These pages provide basic information about sentence structure, parts of speech, paragraph structure, and word choice.

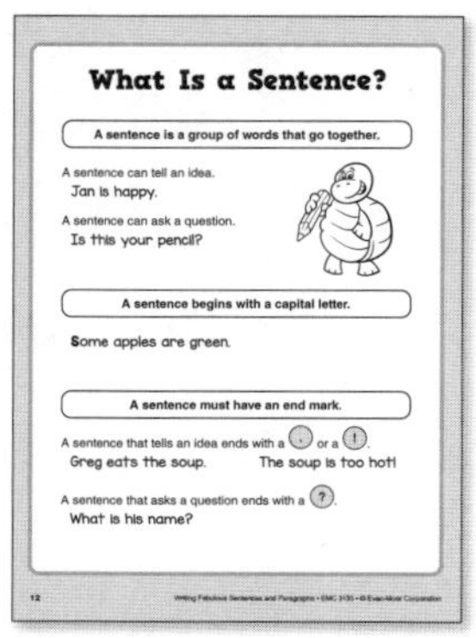

What Is a Sentence?

A sentence is a group of words that go together.

A sentence can tell an idea.
Jan is happy.

A sentence can ask a question.
Is this your pencil?

A sentence begins with a capital letter.

Some apples are green.

A sentence must have an end mark.

A sentence that tells an idea ends with a ⊙ or a ⓘ.
Greg eats the soup. The soup is too hot!

A sentence that asks a question ends with a ⓘ.
What is his name?

Reproduce all of the concept charts for students. Have them staple the pages together to make a sentences-and-paragraphs handbook.

Trait-Based Writing

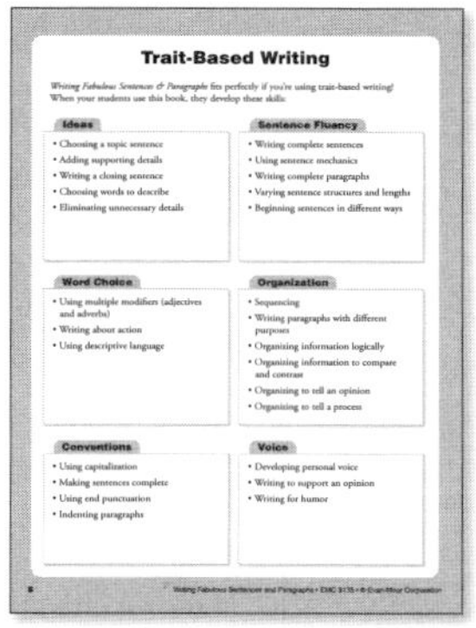
Trait-Based Writing

Ideas	Sentence Fluency

Word Choice	Organization

Conventions	Voice

Page 6 provides a brief overview of trait-based writing, focusing on the six major traits. Use this as a reference for ideas to expand student practice throughout the book.

Forms

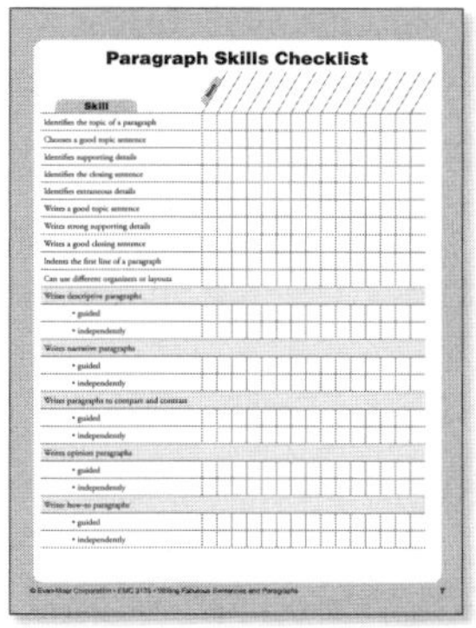
Paragraph Skills Checklist

Paragraph Skills Checklist

Use this checklist on page 7 to track your students' skill progression. Helpful for both student and parent conferences, this list helps you track progress of skills practiced in *Writing Fabulous Sentences & Paragraphs.*

Paragraph Writing Checklist

Make a check ✓ in the box when you have completed the step.

- ☐ 1. Pick a subject for your paragraph.
- ☐ 2. Learn about the subject.
- ☐ 3. Think about what the main idea of the paragraph will be.
- ☐ 4. Write a topic sentence about the main idea.
- ☐ 5. Add supporting details to your paragraph. Does each detail support the main idea?
- ☐ 6. Write a closing sentence about the main idea.
- ☐ 7. Read your paragraph. How can you make it better? Does it make sense?
- ☐ 8. Proofread your paragraph. (You may want to ask a friend to proofread it also.)

Spelling corrected ______

First word indented ______

End punctuation for sentences correct ______

Paragraph Writing Checklist

This checklist on page 8 helps students monitor their own progress while writing a paragraph.

Parts of Speech

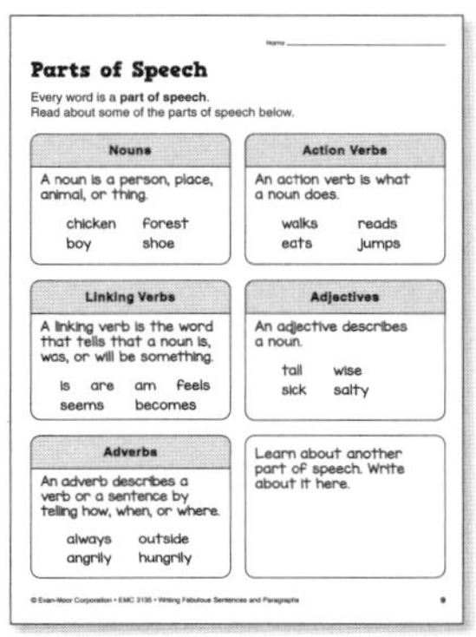
Parts of Speech

Every word is a **part of speech**.
Read about some of the parts of speech below.

Nouns: A noun is a person, place, animal, or thing. chicken, forest, boy, shoe

Action Verbs: An action verb is what a noun does. walks, reads, eats, jumps

Linking Verbs: A linking verb is the word that tells that a noun is, was, or will be something. is, are, am, feels, seems, becomes

Adjectives: An adjective describes a noun. tall, wise, sick, salty

Adverbs: An adverb describes a verb or a sentence by telling how, when, or where. always, outside, angrily, hungrily

Learn about another part of speech. Write about it here.

Page 9 provides a brief overview of basic parts of speech. Reproduce and distribute this page as a guide for students.

Trait-Based Writing

Writing Fabulous Sentences & Paragraphs fits perfectly if you're using trait-based writing! When your students use this book, they develop these skills:

Ideas

- Choosing a topic sentence
- Adding supporting details
- Writing a closing sentence
- Choosing words to describe
- Eliminating unnecessary details

Sentence Fluency

- Writing complete sentences
- Using sentence mechanics
- Writing complete paragraphs
- Varying sentence structures and lengths
- Beginning sentences in different ways

Word Choice

- Using multiple modifiers (adjectives and adverbs)
- Writing about action
- Using descriptive language

Organization

- Sequencing
- Writing paragraphs with different purposes
- Organizing information logically
- Organizing information to compare and contrast
- Organizing to tell an opinion
- Organizing to tell a process

Conventions

- Using capitalization
- Making sentences complete
- Using end punctuation
- Indenting paragraphs

Voice

- Developing personal voice
- Writing to support an opinion
- Writing for humor

Paragraph Skills Checklist

Skill	Name														
Identifies the topic of a paragraph															
Chooses a good topic sentence															
Identifies supporting details															
Identifies the closing sentence															
Identifies extraneous details															
Writes a good topic sentence															
Writes strong supporting details															
Writes a good closing sentence															
Indents the first line of a paragraph															
Can use different organizers or layouts															
Writes descriptive paragraphs															
• guided															
• independently															
Writes narrative paragraphs															
• guided															
• independently															
Writes paragraphs to compare and contrast															
• guided															
• independently															
Writes opinion paragraphs															
• guided															
• independently															
Writes how-to paragraphs															
• guided															
• independently															

Note: Provide students with this checklist to use as they write paragraphs on topics of their own choosing.

Name ____________________

Paragraph Writing Checklist

Make a check ✓ in the box when you have completed the step.

☐ 1. Pick a subject for your paragraph.

☐ 2. Learn about the subject.

☐ 3. Think about what the main idea of the paragraph will be.

☐ 4. Write a topic sentence about the main idea.

☐ 5. Add supporting details to your paragraph.
Does each detail support the main idea?

☐ 6. Write a closing sentence about the main idea.

☐ 7. Read your paragraph.
How can you make it better?
Does it make sense?

☐ 8. Proofread your paragraph.
(You may want to ask a friend to proofread it also.)

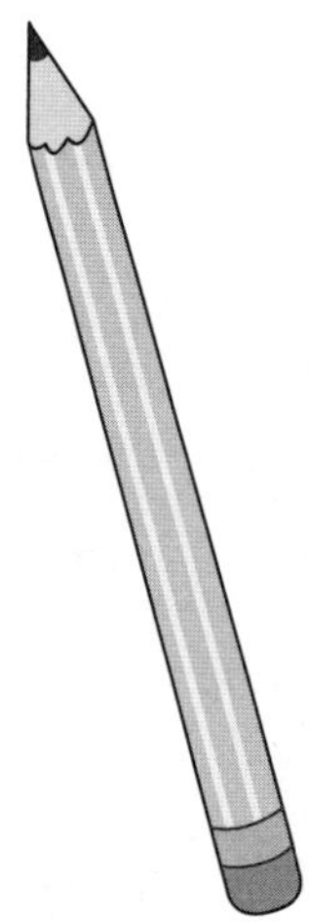

Spelling corrected __________

First word indented __________

End punctuation for sentences correct __________

Name ____________________

Parts of Speech

Every word is a **part of speech**.
Read about some of the parts of speech below.

Nouns

A noun is a person, place, animal, or thing.

chicken forest
boy shoe

Action Verbs

An action verb is what a noun does.

walks reads
eats jumps

Linking Verbs

A linking verb is the word that tells that a noun is, was, or will be something.

is are am feels
seems becomes

Adjectives

An adjective describes a noun.

tall wise
sick salty

Adverbs

An adverb describes a verb or a sentence by telling how, when, or where.

always outside
angrily hungrily

Learn about another part of speech. Write about it here.

Understanding Sentences

What Is a Sentence?

1. Reproduce and distribute to students the **What Is a Sentence?** concept chart on page 12. This chart explains the basics of a sentence. Review the information with students, and have them keep this chart to include in their sentences-and-paragraphs handbook.

2. Pages 13–19 are practice pages that expand on the concepts introduced on the **What Is a Sentence?** chart. These practice pages focus on the following:

    - identifying sentences
    - using sentence mechanics
    - writing sentences correctly
    - completing sentences

    Reproduce and distribute these pages to students.

    Use all of the pages in this section to provide students with scaffolded practice. Or choose pages to use based on the skills you would like to focus on.

A Sentence Has Two Parts

1. Reproduce and distribute to students the **A Sentence Has Two Parts** concept chart on page 20. This chart explains subjects and predicates. Review the information with students, and have them keep this chart to include in their sentences-and-paragraphs handbook.

2. Pages 21–28 are practice pages that expand on the concepts introduced on the **A Sentence Has Two Parts** chart. These practice pages focus on the following:

    - identifying subjects and predicates in sentences
    - writing subjects and predicates
    - writing sentences

    Reproduce and distribute these pages to students.

    Use all of the pages in this section to provide students with scaffolded practice. Or choose pages to use based on the skills you would like to focus on.

Action Verbs and Linking Verbs

1. Reproduce and distribute to students the **Action Verbs and Linking Verbs** concept chart on page 29. This chart shows examples of action verbs and linking verbs in sentences. Review the information with students, and have them keep this chart to include in their sentences-and-paragraphs handbook.

2. Pages 30–33 are practice pages that expand on the concepts introduced on the **Action Verbs and Linking Verbs** chart. These practice pages focus on the following:

   - identifying action verbs and linking verbs
   - writing sentences with different kinds of verbs

   Reproduce and distribute these pages to students.

   Use all of the pages in this section to provide students with scaffolded practice. Or choose pages to use based on the skills you would like to focus on.

Optional: **Expanding on What Is a Sentence?**

- Explain to students that a sentence tells a complete idea. Some groups of words are not sentences. Write examples to show students.
- Explain that you can use either a period or an exclamation point in the same kinds of sentences, but questions must always end with a question mark.

Optional: **Expanding on A Sentence Has Two Parts**

- Explain to students that one easy way to identify the predicate in a sentence is to find the verb. The predicate starts with the verb and usually includes all the words that come after. Show examples.

Optional: **Expanding on Action Verbs and Linking Verbs**

- Explain to students that action verbs tell what someone or something does, while linking verbs tell what someone or something is.
- Have students find examples of action verbs and linking verbs in sentences in books they are reading on their own or as a group.

What Is a Sentence?

A sentence is a group of words that go together.

A sentence can tell an idea.

Jan is happy.

A sentence can ask a question.

Is this your pencil?

A sentence begins with a capital letter.

Some apples are green.

A sentence must have an end mark.

A sentence that tells an idea ends with a (.) or a (!).

Greg eats the soup. The soup is too hot!

A sentence that asks a question ends with a (?).

What is his name?

Name ____________________

Is It a Sentence?

Read the group of words. Is it a sentence? Color **yes** or **no**.

The plate is dirty.

○ yes ○ no

Aunt Sue

○ yes ○ no

some boats

○ yes ○ no

The fish swims in the water.

○ yes ○ no

Uncle Brett waves to me.

○ yes ○ no

at the park

○ yes ○ no

Name ______________________________

A Sentence Begins with a Capital Letter

Read the sentence. Color **yes** if it has a capital letter in the correct place. Color **no** if it does not have a capital letter in the correct place.

the girls Ride their bikes.

○ yes ○ no

The boy kicks the ball.

○ yes ○ no

my friends play a game.

○ yes ○ no

We use a jump rope.

○ yes ○ no

Write a sentence about something you like to do outside. Remember to use a capital letter and an end mark.

____

____

Name ____________________

Tells or Asks?

Read the sentence. Write a (.) or a (!) if it tells an idea.
Write a (?) if it asks a question.

1. Does a zebra have fur ______
2. Do all animals sleep at night ______

3. Tigers can roar loudly ______
4. Roosters are smart animals ______
5. Are frogs smart ______

6. Some animals live on farms ______

Write a sentence that tells about animals.

____

____

Write a question about animals.

____

____

Name ______________________________

Write Capital Letters and End Marks

Read the sentence. It does not have a capital letter. It is missing end marks. Write the sentence correctly on the line. The first one is done for you.

1. the girl puts on her socks

   The girl puts on her socks.

2. can Amar put on his socks

   ____

3. our puppy chews on socks

   ____

4. did you put on your socks

   ____

5. where are my socks

   ____

Name ______________________________

Finish the Sentence and Draw

Read the words. Write any words you want to finish the sentence. Then draw to show what the sentence is about.

1. ______________________________ is in a forest.

2. A kitten ______________________________.

Name ______________________

Write Answers to Questions

Write a sentence to answer each question.
Remember to use a capital letter and an end mark.
The first one is done for you.

1. What is your favorite sport?

   My favorite sport is tennis.

2. What is your favorite snack?

   ____

   ____

3. Where is your favorite place to be?

   ____

   ____

4. What is your favorite color?

   ____

   ____

5. What is your favorite ice cream flavor?

   ____

   ____

Name ___________________________

Wacky Sentences

Read the sentences. They are funny and wacky!

Five furry strawberries run a race.

A little boy jumps over the moon.

Write words to finish the wacky sentences below.
You can use any words in the box or your own words.

beans	bee	boy	carrots	crawl	dance	fish
fruity	hops	moose	runs	slimy	smells	sour

1. These ____________________ taste ____________________.

2. My puppy ____________________ funny.

3. A ____________________ beeped and honked!

4. Can you ____________________ quickly?

A Sentence Has Two Parts

A sentence must have a subject and a predicate.

The **subject** is always a noun.

The **subject** can tell **who does it**.

Ben goes to school.

The **subject** can tell **what does it**.

The wheels turn.

A **predicate** always starts with a verb.

The **predicate** can tell **what happens**.

Pan rides a bike.

The **predicate** can tell **about the subject**.

My milk is cold.

Name ______________________

A Sentence Has a Subject

Read the sentence. The subject is underlined. Color the circle to tell what the subject is. The first one is done for you.

1. <u>A napkin</u> fell on the floor.

○ person ○ place ○ animal ● thing

2. <u>Mindy</u> wipes the table.

○ person ○ place ○ animal ○ thing

3. <u>The kitchen</u> is clean.

○ person ○ place ○ animal ○ thing

4. <u>A bird</u> flew into the house.

○ person ○ place ○ animal ○ thing

5. <u>Chris</u> mops the floor.

○ person ○ place ○ animal ○ thing

Name ______________________________

Find the Subject

Read the sentence. Circle the subject.
The first one is done for you.

1. Mason slides down.
2. A butterfly goes past Maya.
3. The swings look wet today.
4. Eddie jumps in a puddle.
5. The playground is big.
6. A deer walks nearby.

Write a sentence
about being at the playground.
Circle the subject in your sentence.

____

____

Name ____________________

Silly Animal Subjects!

The sentences are silly because the subjects are animals. Write the name of an animal to finish each sentence below. Remember to use a capital letter.

a hamster	a bear	a chicken	the turtle
the eagle	our cat	the parrot	my walrus

1. ______________________________ stirs the soup.

2. ______________________________ talks on the phone.

3. ______________________________ skates at the park.

4. ______________________________ shops at the mall.

Write your own silly sentence about an animal. Remember to use a capital letter and an end mark. Then draw a picture about your sentence.

____

____

____

____

____

Name ______________________

A Sentence Has a Predicate

Read the sentence. The predicate is underlined. Circle the verb. The first one is done for you.

1. Grandma wears an apron.
2. Grandpa fixes the truck.
3. My auntie bakes a pie.
4. The boy feeds the chicks.
5. My cousin paints a picture.
6. My parents rest in the house.
7. Damon rakes leaves.
8. The horse eats hay.
9. Some geese fly in the sky.

Name ______________________________

Find the Predicate

Read the sentence. Then circle the predicate.
The first one is done for you.

1. The dog sniffs the air.
2. Many people take their dogs to the park.
3. My dog's leash is red.
4. Mr. Greco has a new puppy.

5. This dog's fur feels so soft.
6. Adam pets a lot of dogs.

Write a sentence about dogs or cats.
Circle the predicate in your sentence.

____

____

Name ______________________

Find Subjects and Predicates

Read the sentence. Which part is underlined?
Color the circle to tell if it is the **subject** or **predicate**.

1. Tyrone reads five books every month.

○ subject ○ predicate

2. Dana loves the library.

○ subject ○ predicate

3. Mrs. Tree has books in her classroom.

○ subject ○ predicate

4. Dad lost his book.

○ subject ○ predicate

Write a sentence about books.
Then underline the subject in your sentence.
Circle the predicate.

____

____

Name ______________________

Write a Subject or a Predicate

Look at the picture. Then finish the sentences about the picture. Write a subject or predicate.

1. ______________________ is soapy.

2. The girl ______________________.

3. ______________________ are flying.

4. The cat ______________________.

5. ______________________ shines in the sky.

Name ____________________

Write Sentences

Write your own sentences. Use words from the box.
Remember:

☆ a capital letter ☆ an end mark
☆ a subject ☆ a predicate

the mice	the nuts	a firefighter
my friends	a dolphin	dancing
loves baseball	sports	rides a bike
play sports	feeds our pets	wears a hat
my cousins	washes an apple	sharks
puppies	clean their rooms	feels sick

1. ____________________

____

2. ____________________

____

3. ____________________

____

Action Verbs and Linking Verbs

Every sentence has a verb.
A sentence can have an action verb.

Dad flips pancakes.
I pour the syrup.

make	climb	write
ride	run	cook

A sentence can have a linking verb.

Keli is happy.
The kittens are hungry.

am was were

Name ______________________

What Kind of Verb?

Read the sentence. The verb is underlined.
Color the circle to tell if it is an action verb or a linking verb.

I am a soccer player.

○ action

○ linking

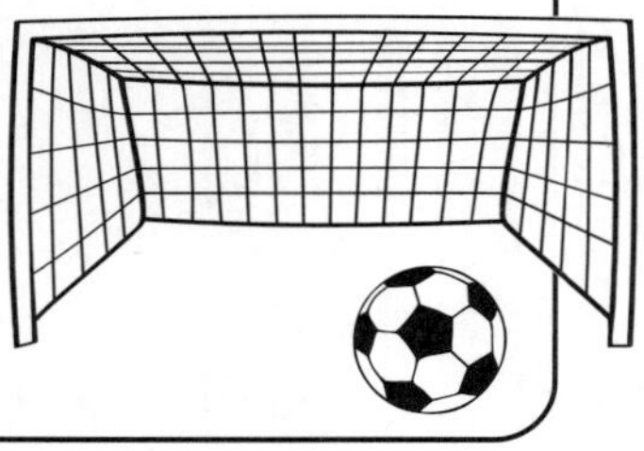

They are baseball players.

○ action

○ linking

The player throws the ball.

○ action

○ linking

The bat makes a loud sound.

○ action

○ linking

Basketball is so fun.

○ action

○ linking

Dory plays golf.

○ action

○ linking

Name ______________________

Action Verbs

Read the sentence. Circle the action verb.
Then write a sentence using the same action verb.

1. The ducks swim in the pond.

____

____

2. The dancer jumps in the air.

____

____

Write a sentence about the ocean that uses an action verb.
Then draw to show what your sentence is about.

____

____

Name ______________________________

Linking Verbs

Read the sentence. Circle the linking verb.
Then write a sentence using the same linking verb.

1. The girl is sad.

____

____

2. The trucks are loud.

____

____

Write a sentence that tells how you feel when you are with your friends. Use a linking verb. Then draw to show what your sentence is about.

____

____

Name ______________________

More Linking Verbs

A linking verb tells about a subject.
These words are linking verbs:

is	are	am	was	were
become	becomes	became	feel	felt
seem	seems	seemed		

Read each sentence about Ricardo and his family. Circle the linking verb.

1. Ricardo is nice.
2. Ricardo's mom felt tired.
3. Ricardo's dad seems strong.
4. Ricardo's brother and sister are funny.

Write a sentence about your family. Use a linking verb in your sentence.

____

____

Writing Fabulous Sentences

You Can Use Adjectives

1. Reproduce and distribute to students the **You Can Use Adjectives** concept chart on page 36. This chart explains that adjectives describe nouns and can make sentences more detailed and interesting to read. Review the information with students, and have them keep this chart to include in their sentences-and-paragraphs handbook.

2. Pages 37–45 are practice pages that expand on the concepts introduced on the **You Can Use Adjectives** chart. These practice pages focus on the following:

    - writing adjectives
    - sensory details
    - using adjectives to describe people

    Reproduce and distribute these pages to students.

    Use all of the pages in this section to provide students with scaffolded practice. Or choose pages to use based on the skills you would like to focus on.

You Can Use Adverbs

1. Reproduce and distribute to students the **You Can Use Adverbs** concept chart on page 46. This chart explains that adverbs in a sentence can describe how, when, or where. Review the information with students, and have them keep this chart to include in their sentences-and-paragraphs handbook.

2. Pages 47–49 are practice pages that expand on the concepts introduced on the **You Can Use Adverbs** chart. These practice pages focus on the following:

    - the function of adverbs in sentences
    - choosing adverbs
    - writing sentences with adverbs

    Reproduce and distribute these pages to students.

    Use all of the pages in this section to provide students with scaffolded practice. Or choose pages to use based on the skills you would like to focus on.

You Can Use New Words

1. Reproduce and distribute to students the **You Can Use New Words** concept chart on page 50. This chart describes ways that students can learn new words. Review the information with students, and have them keep this chart to include in their sentences-and-paragraphs handbook.

2. Pages 51–59 are practice pages that expand on the concept of using new words in sentences, introduced on the **You Can Use New Words** chart. These practice pages focus on the following:

   - word choice
   - parts of speech
   - creative writing

   Reproduce and distribute these pages to students.

   Use all of the pages in this section to provide students with scaffolded practice. Or choose pages to use based on the skills you would like to focus on.

Optional: **Expanding on You Can Use Adjectives**

- Explain to students that adjectives can describe things that you can see and things you cannot see. Talk about character traits with your students to help illustrate examples of adjectives that you cannot see or perceive with the five senses.

Optional: **Expanding on You Can Use Adverbs**

- Explain to students that an adverb can describe a verb, the same way an adjective describes a noun. Write examples to show students.
- Have students find adverbs in books they are reading.

Optional: **Expanding on You Can Use New Words**

- Explain to students that they can learn the meaning of any word they see.
- Practice using a dictionary with your students. Explain that the dictionary is organized in alphabetical order. Ask students to find specific words.
- Explain that students can choose the words they use when they write; explain why word choice is important.

You Can Use Adjectives

Adjectives can tell more about a noun.
Sometimes adjectives make a sentence more fun to read.

James eats a peach. → James eats a **juicy** peach.

I see a garden. → I see a **bright**, **green**, **leafy** garden.

There are bugs here! → There are **five huge** bugs here!

Adjectives can help "show" what a noun looks like.

My grandma has **curly black hair**, **long** fingernails, and **brown eyes**.

The playground has a **giant** slide and a **wobbly** bridge.

Name ____________________

Add Adjectives

Finish the sentence. Write an adjective from the box on the line.

cold	colorful	funny	happy	nice	old
pretty	scary	slimy	sour	sweet	weird

1. Avery wants to watch a ____________________ movie.

2. Simone's puppy is ____________________.

3. This bakery smells ____________________.

4. I feel ____________________ when I wear my sweater.

5. Grandma's house is ____________________.

6. The rocks in the yard are ____________________.

Write a sentence about your bedroom. Use an adjective.

____

____

Name ______________________

What You See

Adjectives can tell about what you **see**.
You can write to tell what something looks like.

What is your favorite place that is outside? Write it.

____

Write three adjectives to tell what this place looks like.

______________ ______________ ______________

Write a sentence that tells what this place looks like.
Use one of the adjectives that you wrote.

____

____

Draw a picture of your favorite outside place.

Name ______________________

What You Hear

Adjectives can tell about what you **hear**.
You can write to tell what something sounds like.

Circle one place you have been to.

zoo beach park forest

Write three adjectives to tell what this place sounds like.

______________ ______________ ______________

Write a sentence that tells what this place sounds like.
Use one of the adjectives that you wrote.

____

____

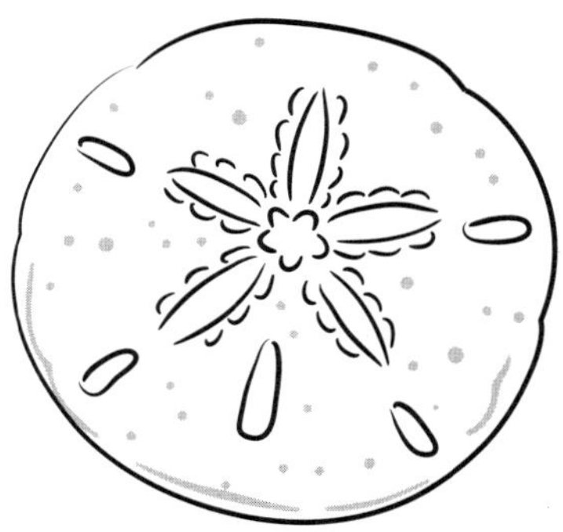

Name ____________________

What You Smell

Adjectives can tell about what you **smell**.
You can write to tell what something smells like.

Circle one of these places.

your favorite restaurant   your kitchen   school lunch room

Write three adjectives to tell what this place smells like.

____________________ ____________________ ____________________

Write a sentence that tells what this place smells like.
Use one of the adjectives that you wrote.

____

____

Name ______________________________

What You Taste

Adjectives can tell about what you **taste**.
You can write to tell what something tastes like.

What is one of your favorite foods? Write it.

____

Write three adjectives to tell what this food tastes like.

______________ ______________ ______________

Write a sentence that tells what this food tastes like.
Use one of the adjectives that you wrote.

____

____

Draw a picture of this food.

Name ______________________________

How You Feel

Adjectives can tell about how you feel.
You can write to tell how you feel on the inside.

Write a sentence to answer each question.
Use an adjective from the box in each sentence.

cheerful	happy	loved	mad	okay
sad	shy	surprised	thankful	upset

1. How do you feel when a friend does not want to play with you?

____

____

2. How do you feel when your mom makes your favorite lunch?

____

____

3. How does your dad feel when you give him a hug?

____

____

Name ______________________

What Do You Look Like?

You can write to tell what any person looks like. Mario wrote about himself. Read what Mario wrote.

I have brown hair.
It is curly.
I am short.
I have big eyes.
My fingers are pointy.

You can write to tell about yourself!
Write 5 sentences that tell what you look like.
Use an adjective in each sentence.

1. ______________________________

____

2. ______________________________

____

3. ______________________________

____

4. ______________________________

____

5. ______________________________

____

Name ______________________

What You Touch or Feel

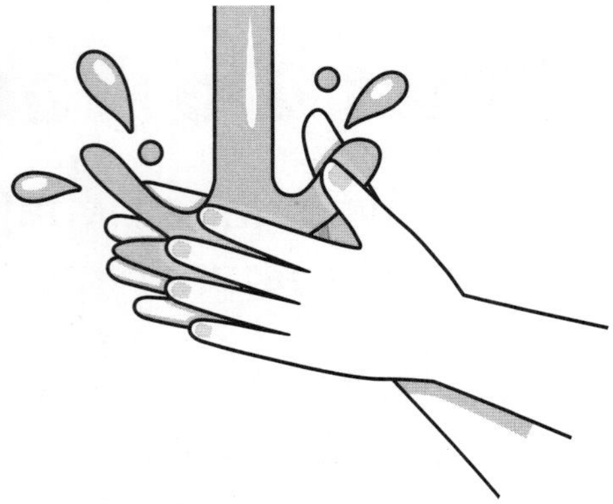

Adjectives can tell about what you **touch or feel**.
You can write to tell what something feels like.

Circle one of these things.

a rock   a blanket   water   a leaf

Write three adjectives to tell what this thing feels like.

______________ ______________ ______________

Write a sentence that tells what this thing feels like.
Use one of the adjectives that you wrote.

____

____

Draw a picture of something you like to touch or feel.

Name ______________________

Write About Somebody You Know

Bashar wrote sentences about his mom.
Then he drew a picture of her.
Read what Bashar wrote.

My mom is smart.

My mom is tall.

She has green eyes.

She is very kind.

Think of somebody you know.
Write three sentences about this person.
Use adjectives in your sentences.

Remember, you can write about what this person is like on the inside, too!

1. ____

____

2. ____

____

3. ____

____

You Can Use Adverbs

Adverbs can tell **how** or **when** or **where**.
You can write sentences with adverbs.

how

Sara chews **slowly**.
Veeda reads **quietly**.

when

Amy will arrive **soon**.
Kaito will leave **later**.

where

The birds sing **beautifully**.
The crab crawls **around**.

Name ____________________

What Does the Adverb Tell?

Read the sentence. Then color to show if the adverb tells **how**, **when**, or **where**.

Horatio puts on his jacket **cheerfully**.

○ how ○ when ○ where

Angel will call his grandpa **later**.

○ how ○ when ○ where

The bird builds a nest **carefully**.

○ how ○ when ○ where

Malik climbs **up**.

○ how ○ when ○ where

Hana cuts the sandwich **evenly**.

○ how ○ when ○ where

Name ______________________________

Choose an Adverb

Read the sentence. Choose an adverb to finish the sentence.
Write the adverb on the line.

1. Alex ____________________ plays the piano.
   quietly   loudly

2. "Did you go into my room?" Morgan asked ____________________.
   angrily   nicely

3. The fish swim ____________________.
   badly   well

4. Andrea ____________________ throws the ball into the hoop.
   happily   wildly

5. Uncle Daryll ____________________ made himself a sandwich.
   hungrily   slowly

6. Jayque ____________________ makes his bed.
   neatly   poorly

Write a sentence about getting ready for school.
Use an adverb in your sentence.

____

____

Name ______________________________

Write Sentences with Adverbs

Read the adverbs in the boxes.

how	when	where
closely	today	below
proudly	tomorrow	above
gently	everyday	far
loudly	anytime	here
slowly	sometimes	there
quickly	then	outside
bravely	after	around

Write a sentence. Use an adverb that tells **how**.

____

____

Write a sentence. Use an adverb that tells **when**.

____

____

Write a sentence. Use an adverb that tells **where**.

____

____

You Can Use New Words

You may hear someone say a new word.

You may read a new word in a book.

You can use the new words you learn to write fabulous sentences.

Name ____________________

New Verbs Are Fun!

Read the word meaning and look at the picture. Then read the sentence. Write a sentence of your own using the same word.

crawl  to move on your hands and knees	You can **crawl** on the floor. ______ ______ ______
spy  to see something	I **spy** a bird in a tree. ______ ______ ______
roar  to let out a loud cry or a loud sound	The lion let out a **roar**. ______ ______ ______

Name ____________________

New Adjectives Are Fun!

Read the word meaning and look at the picture. Then read the sentence. Write a sentence of your own using the same word.

timid  feeling shy around other people	Shelly feels **timid** at school sometimes. ____________________ ____________________ ____________________
thrilled  very excited	I am **thrilled** to try the cookies that my dad baked. ____________________ ____________________ ____________________
bumpy  to have lumps sticking out	The toad's skin feels rough because it is **bumpy**. ____________________ ____________________ ____________________

Name ______________________________

New Nouns Are Fun!

Read the word meaning and look at the picture. Then read the sentence. Write a sentence of your own using the same word.

shore

the land next to sea or water

There is a starfish on the **shore**.

____

____

____

vehicle

something people drive

My dad's favorite **vehicle** is his truck.

____

____

____

mural

a big painting on a wall

Juan's school has a **mural** in the lunch room.

____

____

____

Name ____________________

New Words Are Awesome!

Read the words. Color the shape if you have never seen or heard the word before.

cling pause peer shabby host

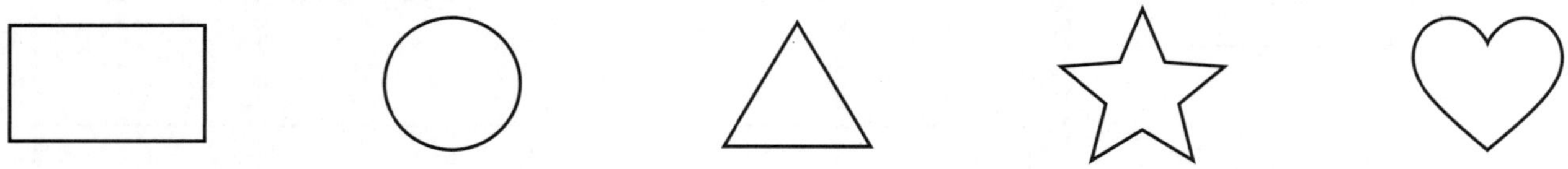

Read the chart.

Word	What it means	Sentence
cling	to hold on tightly	The baby monkey clings to her mom.
pause	to stop or wait for a short time	Pause the movie for a minute.
peer	a friend or someone who is the same as you in some ways	My classmates are my peers.
shabby	broken, dirty, or worn out	My old shoes look shabby.
host	a person who invites people over to have fun	I am the host of my birthday party.

Write a sentence. Use a word from the chart.

____

____

Name ______________________________

Finish the Story!

Read the story. Write a word on each line to finish the story.

Drake is hiking with his ________________.
family friends

They are walking through a ________________.
jungle forest

Drake sees ________________ trees.
tall green

Drake and Franky stop walking and take a ________________.
break rest

Then everyone heard a ________________ crash.
powerful loud

Sage said that a tree branch had fallen. She told everybody

to be very ________________ on the hike.
watchful careful

Drake thought that the hike was so ________________.
interesting scary

Name ______________________________

Finish the Sentences!

Uh-oh! Some of the words in the story are missing.
Write words from the box to finish the sentences.

adored	amazing	dress	fabulous	goofy	great
jacket	jiggled	liked	loved	scarf	shirt
stylish	suit	twisted	unusual	weird	wiggled

Sheena, the Fabulous Penguin

Some of the other penguins thought Sheena was

______________ when she started to wear hats. The polar bears laughed when they saw Sheena wear

a ______________. "How ______________ she is," they said.

One day, Sheena saw a ______________ that she

wanted to wear. She ______________ how it looked. "Do not wear that!" said the seals and orcas. "It's not for you!"

Sheena did not listen. She ______________ her body into the outfit until it fit. When Sheena finally wore it, she looked in the mirror.

"Wow, I look ______________," she thought. Sheena wore everything she loved, all the time.

Name ____________________

Write Fabulous Sentences!

Write a sentence that tells what your favorite movie is. Then draw a picture of your favorite character in the movie.

____

____

____

____

____

____

Write a sentence about your family. Then draw a picture of your family.

____

____

____

____

____

____

Name ______________________________

More Fabulous Sentences!

Write a sentence to tell what your favorite animal is.

____

____

Why is this animal your favorite?
Write a sentence to tell why.
Then draw a picture of the animal.

____

____

____

If you could meet someone who is famous, who would it be?
Write a sentence to tell about him or her.

____

____

Write one question you could ask this famous person.
Remember to use a question mark.

____

____

Name ______________________________

Fun and Fabulous Sentences!

Write a fabulous sentence about each picture.
Use an adjective or adverb! Then color the picture.

____
____
____
____

____
____
____
____

____
____
____
____

Understanding Paragraphs

What Is a Paragraph?

1. Reproduce and distribute to students the **What Is a Paragraph?** concept chart on page 62. This chart explains the basics of a paragraph. Review the information with students. Point out that the first sentence is indented to show the start of a new paragraph. Have students keep this chart to include in their sentences-and-paragraphs handbook.

2. Pages 63–65 are practice pages that expand on the concepts introduced on the **What Is a Paragraph?** chart. These practice pages focus on the following:

    - identifying paragraphs
    - recognizing indented sentences
    - understanding that all sentences in a paragraph must be related

    Reproduce and distribute these pages to students.

    Use all of the pages in this section to provide students with scaffolded practice. Or choose pages to use based on the skills you would like to focus on.

A Paragraph Has Three Parts

1. Reproduce and distribute to students the **A Paragraph Has Three Parts** concept chart on page 66. This chart explains that paragraphs have a topic sentence, supporting details, and a closing sentence. Review the information with students, and have them keep this chart to include in their sentences-and-paragraphs handbook.

2. Pages 67–87 are practice pages that expand on the concepts introduced on the **A Paragraph Has Three Parts** chart. These practice pages focus on the following:

    - identifying parts of a paragraph
    - writing topic sentences
    - writing supporting details
    - writing closing sentences

    Reproduce and distribute these pages to students.

    Use all of the pages in this section to provide students with scaffolded practice. Or choose pages to use based on the skills you would like to focus on.

Optional: **Expanding on What Is a Paragraph?**

- Explain to students that paragraphs can be long or short. Explain that paragraphs can have fewer than five sentences or more than five sentences.
- Have students find a paragraph in a book they are reading individually or as a class. Ask students to explain how they know it is a paragraph.

Optional: **Expanding on A Paragraph Has Three Parts**

- Explain to students that the topic sentence is often the first sentence in a paragraph, but not always.
- Create a paragraph as a whole group!

  Step 1: Write a topic sentence on the board or where all students can read it. (See topic sentence suggestions below.)

  Step 2: Each student takes a turn adding a new sentence to make a paragraph. (You may need to write more than one topic sentence and create more than one paragraph so that all students have a turn collaborating on a paragraph.) Encourage students to be creative with their sentences!

  Step 3: When everyone has had a turn writing, read all the paragraphs aloud as a group!

Suggestions for Topic Sentences

- Music is important.
- The world would be different without television or computers.
- There are many different ways to dance.
- It would be fun to be a superhero with superpowers.
- There are many things I like to do in winter.

What Is a Paragraph?

A paragraph is a group of sentences that go together.

All of the sentences in a paragraph are about one main topic or one main idea. This is a paragraph:

There are many ways to eat an apple. You can hold an apple and take bites out of it. Another way is to cut the apple and put peanut butter on it. You can also chop an apple and put it on oatmeal. These are just some of the ways that you can eat an apple.

The first sentence in a paragraph is always indented.

That means there is a big space before the first sentence starts.

Name ______________________________

Is It a Paragraph?

Read the words. Then color **yes** if it is a paragraph. Color **no** if it is not.

Janet slowly gets ready for school.

○ yes ○ no

Pedro gets ready for school. He brushes his teeth. He puts on his clothes. He puts books in his backpack. He is ready for school.

○ yes ○ no

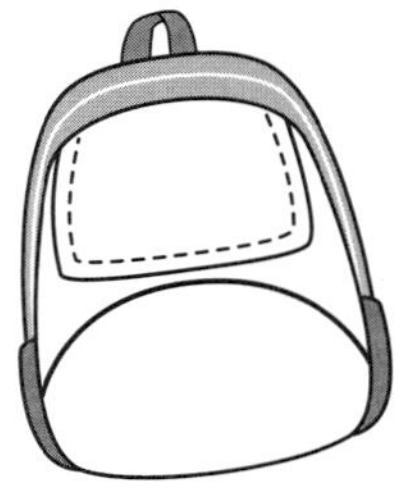

Pam will wear her new shoes to school.

○ yes ○ no

Lacy likes to wait at the bus stop. She sees her friend Luke there. Lacy likes to watch the bus as it comes closer. She likes being outside. Lacy always feels cheerful at the bus stop.

○ yes ○ no

Name ______________________________

Is the Sentence Indented?

The first sentence of a paragraph needs to be indented.

Read the paragraph. Then write **yes** if the paragraph is indented. Write **no** if the paragraph is not indented.

    This is how Rosemary makes her yogurt snack. First, she puts vanilla yogurt in a bowl. Second, she puts in berries and banana slices. Third, she pours some honey on top. Then her yogurt snack is ready to eat.

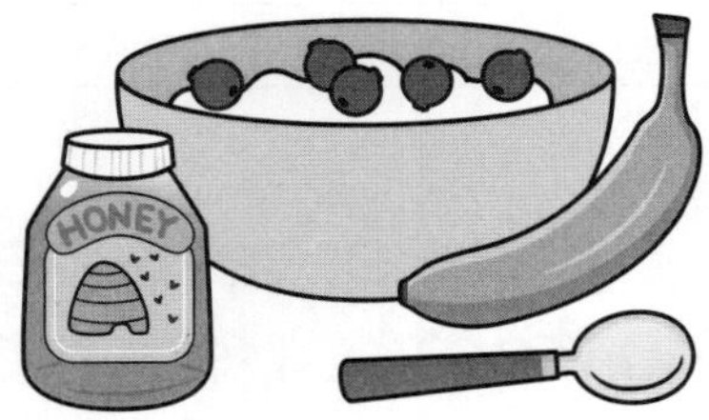

____

The ocean has many animals. Sharks live in the ocean. Whales are ocean animals, too. Eels live in the ocean. Many other animals also live in the ocean.

____

    Roses can be different colors. There are red roses. There are white ones. There are also pink ones. Roses can be even more colors, too.

____

Name ____________________

Do the Sentences Go Together?

All the sentences in a paragraph should be about one main topic or one main idea. Read the paragraph.

Color **yes** if the sentences go together.

Color **no** if the sentences do not go together.

I think Saturday is the best day of the week. I am glad there is no school on Saturday. Also, my family watches football every Saturday. I play outside with my friends on Saturday. Saturday is better than any other day!

yes **no**

There are different kinds of bears. There are polar bears, grizzly bears, and black bears. Penguins are birds that do not fly. Spiders are not insects. Can you name different kinds of bears?

yes **no**

Reggie likes to do art. He has paintbrushes and paints. He also uses clay to make art. Reggie likes using his markers to draw, too. There are lots of ways Reggie makes art.

yes **no**

A Paragraph Has Three Parts

A paragraph has a **topic sentence**, **supporting details**, and a **closing sentence**.

Part 1: Topic Sentence

The topic sentence tells the main idea of the paragraph.

David reads a lot. He reads ten books every month. He has read over a hundred books. He reads every day. David reads as much as he can.

Part 2: Supporting Details

The supporting details tell more about the main idea.

David reads a lot. **He reads ten books every month. He has read over a hundred books. He reads every day.** David reads as much as he can.

Part 3: Closing Sentence

The closing sentence retells the topic sentence in a different way.

David reads a lot. He reads ten books every month. He has read over a hundred books. He reads every day. **David reads as much as he can.**

Name ____________________

Topic Sentence

A paragraph has a topic sentence.
It tells the main idea, or what the paragraph is about.

Read the paragraph. Circle the topic sentence.
The first one is done for you.

Sometimes I wish that I could fly. I would fly with the birds. I would fly to a mountaintop. I would look down at the cars and buildings from the sky. I wish I could fly right now!

Meena learned how to ride a bike. She practiced riding without falling. She learned how to stop the bike safely. Her dad showed her how to turn the bike. Meena knows how to ride a bike now.

Mike's favorite food is soup. He likes every flavor of soup. Mike eats noodle soup a lot. His mom makes him tomato soup every week. Even though Mike likes other foods, too, soup is what he likes best.

Alicia's family gave some of their things to a place that helps people. The family gave shoes and clothes. Alicia and her brother gave some toys. Her parents gave some pots and pans. Alicia's family gave things because they wanted to help people who might need them.

Name ____________________

Match the Topic Sentence

Uh-oh! The topic sentence is missing from each paragraph. Draw a line to match each topic sentence to a paragraph.

He would rather read a book than play sports. He gets bored when he plays. He does not even like watching sports games. There are a lot of things that Josh likes to do, but playing sports is not one of them. •

• Omar likes basketball.

She likes to see animals such as owls when she camps. She likes to roast marshmallows on the campfire. She thinks it is fun to put up the tent. Allie likes camping a lot! •

• Josh does not like sports.

He has a small basketball hoop in his bedroom. He went to basketball camp last summer. He plays basketball with his friends. He wishes he could play basketball all the time! •

• Allie thinks camping is fun.

Name ____________________

Choose the Topic Sentence

Uh-oh! The topic sentence is missing from each paragraph. Read each paragraph. Then color the ☆ next to the best topic sentence.

She called the restaurant. She asked for extra cheese and olives. She also said that she wanted the crust to be thin. Shanice could not wait to eat the pizza she ordered.

Which is the best topic sentence?

☆ Shanice ate a pizza.

☆ Shanice ordered a pizza.

Craig gives his dog a bath. Then he brushes his dog's fur. Craig gives his dog a healthy meal. Craig loves taking care of his dog.

Which is the best topic sentence?

☆ Craig takes good care of his dog.

☆ Craig does not like to care for his dog.

Britney likes unicorns, and Selena does, too. Both girls like to drink banana milk. They are both in second grade. They are the same in some ways.

Which is the best topic sentence?

☆ Britney and Selena are alike.

☆ Britney and Selena are classmates.

Name ____________________

Finish the Topic Sentence

Read the paragraph. Part of the topic sentence is missing. Write to finish the topic sentence. The first one is done for you.

Dogs can eat many foods that people can also eat. Dogs can eat carrots and broccoli. Dogs can eat meat. Many dogs like to eat sweet potatoes. There are many other foods that both people and dogs can eat.

There are three things I do ____________________. I put on a sweater or a jacket. I use a blanket. I drink something warm like hot chocolate. These things always make me feel warmer when I feel cold.

There are a lot of ____________________. One flavor is banana. Another flavor is strawberry. Many people also like peanut butter in their milkshakes. There are so many milkshake flavors, and you can try them all!

Name ______________________

A Better Topic Sentence

Read the paragraph. It is missing a topic sentence.
Choose a topic sentence for the paragraph.

____.

Some families have only one kid. Some families have more than one kid. Some families have people who look alike, and some families have people who look different. There are so many families, and they are different from each other.

Which topic sentence works better in this paragraph? Color the star.

☆ Families can be different.

☆ All families are exactly the same.

____.

Some people choose to play the piano. Some people would rather play the drums. Other people may want to play the flute. There are many ways to play music.

Which topic sentence works better in this paragraph? Color the star.

☆ People can choose how they want to play music.

☆ There is only one way for people to play music.

Name ____________________

Supporting Details

A paragraph has supporting details. The details tell more about the main idea. Read the paragraph. Underline three sentences that have supporting details. The first one is done for you.

Abdul does chores after school. First, he puts away his backpack and shoes. Second, he sweeps the kitchen floor. Third, he helps his dad cook dinner. It does not take long for Abdul to do his chores after school.

Some animals are called a different name when they are babies. Baby frogs are called tadpoles. Baby cows are called calves. Baby kangaroos are called joeys. There are more animals with different baby names, too.

Ashley and her cousin Dana are so different. Ashley likes baseball best, and Dana likes hockey best. Ashley likes to wear jeans, and Dana likes to wear leggings. Ashley likes pasta, but Dana does not like pasta at all. Ashley and Dana are cousins, but they are not alike.

Name ____________________

Match Supporting Details

Read the topic sentence.

Topic Sentence:

Fish make good pets.

The topic sentence tells the main idea. Color the stars next to three sentences that tell more about the main idea.

☆ They follow you around your house because they love you.

☆ They can bark, do tricks, and play games with you.

☆ They are quiet.

☆ You can pet their fur.

☆ It is fun to watch them swim.

☆ They are neat pets that do not make a mess in your house.

Name ____________________

Match More Supporting Details

Read the topic sentence.

Topic Sentence:

Jill likes math.

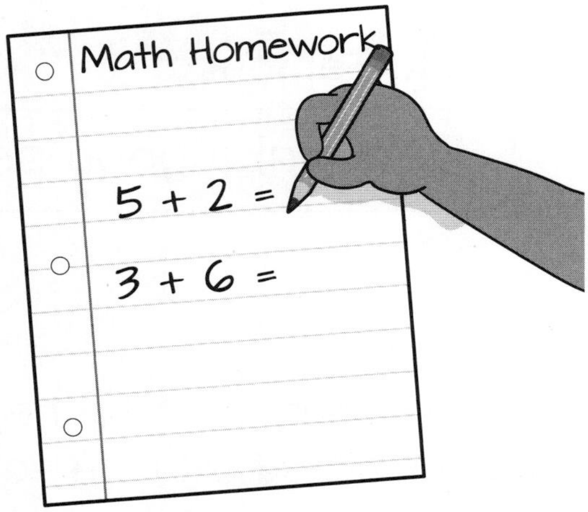

The topic sentence tells the main idea. Color the stars next to three sentences that tell more about the main idea.

☆ She looks for numbers everywhere she goes.

☆ She does not like numbers.

☆ She likes to add numbers together to find a sum.

☆ Jill does not like adding or subtracting numbers.

☆ She never wants to solve a math problem ever again.

☆ Jill also likes to do subtraction.

Name ______________________

Choose the Supporting Detail

Uh-oh! A supporting detail is missing from each paragraph. Read each paragraph. Then color the ☆ next to the best supporting detail.

Uncle Sal is funny. He plays funny pranks on our whole family. He tries to make people laugh. ______________________. Uncle Sal is one of the funniest people I know.

Which is the best supporting detail for this paragraph?

☆ He tells funny jokes.

☆ He told a sad story once.

Some people think koalas look cute. Koalas have fluffy fur, so they look cuddly. They are quite small. ______________________. Even though koalas are wild animals, some people think they're cute and cuddly.

Which is the best supporting detail for this paragraph?

☆ Koalas live in trees.

☆ Koalas have big round eyes.

Name ______________________________

Write a Supporting Detail

Look at the picture and read the paragraph.
Then write one more supporting detail.

Selma and her friends are at the pool. Selma and Cole play with a beach ball. Paco uses his feet to splash water at Pippa.

____

____

______________________________.

Selma and her friends are having fun!

Name ____________________

Which Sentence Does Not Belong?

Read the paragraph. Cross out the supporting detail that does not belong.

Rats are smart animals. They can remember things well. They can talk to each other with sounds. Some people think mice are cute. Rats have brains and can learn because they are smart.

Honey bees make the honey that we eat. They find flowers and collect nectar. A honey bee's stomach helps change the nectar into honey. Sometimes you can find bird nests in trees. People collect the honey that honey bees make.

Popcorn is a snack made from real corn kernels. When a corn kernel gets hot, its skin breaks and pops. A lot of people like to eat candy when they watch a movie. After the corn pops, some people add butter and salt to their popcorn. If you like real corn kernels, you might like popcorn.

Name ______________________________

A Better Supporting Detail

Read the paragraph. It is missing a supporting detail. Choose a supporting detail for the paragraph.

People do a lot of different jobs. Some people work in a hospital as a doctor or a nurse. Some people are teachers, cleaners, or chefs.

____.

There are so many jobs that a person could choose to do.

Which supporting detail works better in this paragraph? Color the star.

☆ Most people like to watch movies.

☆ Some people work as firefighters.

Marco gets his soccer uniform ready for the game. First, he helps his mom wash the uniform. Second, Marco checks the uniform for loose strings or wrinkles.

____.

Now his uniform is ready for his next game.

Which supporting detail works better in this paragraph? Color the star.

☆ Third, he lays his full uniform out on his dresser.

☆ Then Marco eats breakfast before the game.

Name ______________________

Think of Supporting Details

Read the topic sentences. Write the supporting details for each one.

Reading about animals is fun.

1. ______________________
2. ______________________
3. ______________________

There are a lot of yummy breakfast foods.

1. ______________________
2. ______________________
3. ______________________

There are different ways to be a good friend.

1. ______________________
2. ______________________
3. ______________________

Name ____________________

Closing Sentence

A paragraph has a closing sentence. It retells the main idea, or what the paragraph is about, in a different way. Read the paragraph. Circle the closing sentence. The first one is done for you.

Pearl wears her favorite shirt as much as she can. She wears it to school. She wears it on the weekends. She even wears it when she goes to her grandma's house to visit. Pearl would wear her favorite shirt every day if she could!

Hank does a lot of exercise. Sometimes he runs or jogs. Sometimes he uses a jump rope. On other days, he rides his bike with his dad. Hank exercises every day.

Ava wants a pet fox. She thinks foxes are cute. She thinks a fox would be a good pet because foxes are smart. Ava also learned that foxes can be loving and loyal. Ava told her parents that she would do anything for a pet fox.

The Bradley family likes to make salads. Sometimes they put kale in their salads. Sometimes they put seeds in their salads. They even put fruit in their salads! Salads are one of the family's favorite foods to make.

Name ____________________

Match the Closing Sentence

Uh-oh! The closing sentence is missing from each paragraph. Draw a line to match each closing sentence to a paragraph.

It was such a hot day, and Toya wanted to feel cooler. She put ice cubes in water and drank it. Then she put on a shirt with short sleeves. Last, she turned on the fan.	• •	If Mrs. Loop sees a rock anywhere, she will collect it.
This video game is awesome! The characters in the game look so real. The game's story is fun to play. And the game music is cool.	• •	Toya felt cooler after everything she did.
Mrs. Loop collects rocks. She gather rocks at the beach. She picks up rocks in the forest. She has even found rocks at the park.	• •	I want to show this game to my friends because I like it so much!

Name ____________________

Choose the Closing Sentence

Uh-oh! The closing sentence is missing from each paragraph. Read each paragraph. Then color the ☆ next to the best closing sentence.

Cars and bikes are the same in some ways. They both have wheels. They both have seats that people can sit on. And they both have a part that the driver holds onto and uses to turn.

Which is the best closing sentence?

☆ These are just a few ways that cars and bikes are alike.

☆ These are just a few ways that cars and bikes are different.

My Aunt Maria has a service dog named Max. Aunt Maria is blind, and Max helps her when she goes places. Max is a good listener and does whatever she tells him to do. Max is a sweet and gentle dog.

Which is the best closing sentence?

☆ There are so many different dog breeds.

☆ Max is a really great dog.

Name ____________________

Finish the Closing Sentence

Read the paragraph. Finish the closing sentence.
The first one is done for you.

Books and movies are the same in some ways. They both tell a story. They have a beginning, a middle, and an end. They both can make people laugh. These are some ways that books and movies are the same.

I can't wait to go to the carnival this weekend! My brother and I want to go on all the rides. We will also play games and try to win a prize! Then we plan to get some yummy snacks at the carnival. ____________________ to be at the carnival this weekend!

There are lots of things you can do to help people who live in your town. You can help walk people's dogs. Another thing you can do is read to people. You can give away some things that you do not use. ____________________ to help people in your town.

Name ______________________

A Better Closing Sentence

Read the paragraph. It is missing a closing sentence.
Choose words to finish the closing sentence for the paragraph.

People use different foods to make healthy smoothies. Some people make smoothies out of just fruits and vegetables. Some people add spices or other flavors to their smoothies. Some people use oatmeal, peanut butter, or other foods. You can ______________________.

Which words work better for the closing sentence?
Color the star.

☆ make a smoothie with almost any foods

☆ drink a smoothie in the morning or at night

Recycling can help take care of the planet. When we recycle, there is less garbage. Earth stays cleaner. Animals don't get sick from so much garbage. ______________________ to help the planet stay clean and safe.

Which words work better for the closing sentence?
Color the star.

☆ You can adopt a pet

☆ Many people recycle

Name ____________________

Write Sentences Together

Read the topic and the details below. Think of a topic sentence about sloths. Write it. Then write sentences that support the topic sentence. Write a closing sentence.

Sloths

- can have two toes or three toes
- are mammals
- live in rainforests
- spend most of their time hanging in trees

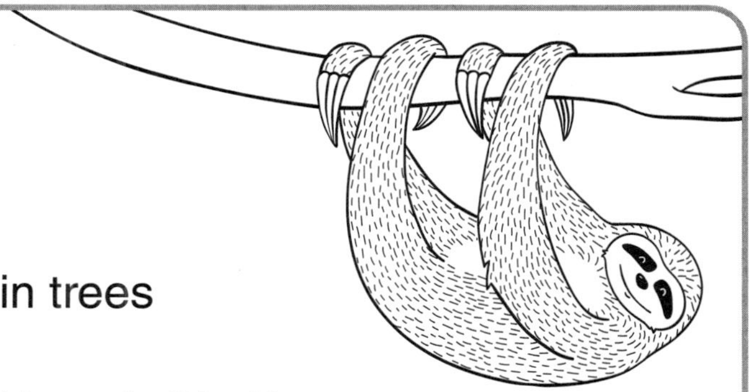

My Paragraph About Sloths

Name ______________________

Write More Sentences Together

Read the topic and the details below. Think of a topic sentence about table tennis and tennis. Write it. Then write sentences that support the topic sentence. Write a closing sentence.

Table Tennis and Tennis

- use a ball
- are played by hitting the ball
- have a net
- can be played with only two people

My Paragraph About Table Tennis and Tennis

____

____

____

____

____

____

____

____

____

____

Name ______________________________

Write and Put Sentences Together

Read the topic and the details below. Think of a topic sentence about plums. Write it. Then write sentences that support the topic sentence. Write a closing sentence.

Plums

- are fruits
- can be different colors
- have vitamin C
- taste sweet

My Paragraph About Plums

____

____

____

____

____

____

____

____

____

____

Writing Fabulous Paragraphs

Different Kinds of Paragraphs

1. Reproduce and distribute to students the **Different Kinds of Paragraphs** concept chart on page 90. This chart explains that there are different kinds of paragraphs with different purposes. Review the information with students, and have them keep this chart to include in their sentences-and-paragraphs handbook.

Opinion Paragraph

Pages 91 and 92 let students practice writing opinion paragraphs. First, distribute page 91 to students and have them complete the activity. Then distribute page 92 to students. Instruct them to use Tyson's paragraph as a guide as they complete page 92.

Compare Paragraph

Pages 93 and 94 let students practice writing paragraphs that compare. First, distribute page 93 to students and have them complete the activity. Then distribute page 94 to students. Instruct them to use Erica's paragraph as a guide as they complete page 94.

Contrast Paragraph

Pages 95 and 96 let students practice writing paragraphs that contrast. First, distribute page 95 to students and have them complete the activity. Then distribute page 96 to students. Instruct them to use Mike's paragraph as a guide as they complete page 96.

Narrative Paragraph

Pages 97 and 98 let students practice writing narrative paragraphs. First, distribute page 97 to students and have them complete the activity. Then distribute page 98 to students. Instruct them to use Briana's paragraph as a guide as they complete page 98.

Descriptive Paragraph

Pages 99 and 100 let student practice writing descriptive paragraphs. First, distribute page 99 to students and have them complete the activity. Then distribute page 100 to students. Instruct them to use Tanya's paragraph as a guide as they complete page 100.

How-to Paragraph

Pages 101 and 102 let students practice writing how-to paragraphs. First, distribute page 101 to students and have them complete the activity. Then distribute page 102 to students. Instruct them to use Trevor's paragraph as a guide as they complete page 102.

2. Pages 103–109 are practice pages that each further expand on the concepts introduced on the **Different Kinds of Paragraphs** chart. These practice pages focus on the following:

   - writing different kinds of paragraphs
   - writing topic sentences, supporting details, and closing sentences

   Reproduce and distribute these pages to students.

   Use all of the activities in this section to provide students with scaffolded practice. Or choose activities to use based on the skills you would like to focus on.

Optional: **Expanding on Different Kinds of Paragraphs**

- Point out to students that a paragraph that compares tells how two people or things are the same. Explain that a paragraph that contrasts tells how two people or things are different. And then explain to students that a paragraph can do both, by telling how two people or things are the same and different.
- Remind students that a descriptive paragraph can tell about anything, including people, places, animals, or things. It can even tell about things we cannot see or perceive with our five senses.
- Have students find different kinds of paragraphs in news articles, online, in books, and in other materials with text. Ask students to tell what kind of paragraphs they are.
- Have a whole-group discussion about an issue or topic that your students have opinions about. After discussing different viewpoints and angles of the topic, have students write an opinion paragraph stating their own opinions.
- Make a healthy snack or make something as a whole group. Then have students write a paragraph explaining how to make it.

Different Kinds of Paragraphs

Writing paragraphs can be fun when you write about different topics.

You can write about things that are real or things that are pretend.

- ☆ You can write a paragraph about things you do.
- ☆ You can write a paragraph about what you think.
- ☆ You can write a paragraph about how two things are the same or different.
- ☆ You can write a paragraph about things that are pretend.

Name ______________________________

Read Tyson's Paragraph

An Opinion Paragraph

Tyson wrote a paragraph about something he likes. Read Tyson's paragraph.

I like comic books. Comic books have a lot of pictures for me to look at. Comic books are easy for me to read. I like that comic books are not very long. I like comic books because they are fun to read.

Write the topic sentence from Tyson's paragraph.

Write one supporting detail sentence from Tyson's paragraph.

Write the closing sentence from Tyson's paragraph.

Name ______________________________

Something That You Like

An Opinion Paragraph

Write a paragraph about something you like. You can write about anything. Use Tyson's paragraph to help you.

One thing that I really like is ______________________________

____.

I like how ____

____.

Also, ____

____.

Another reason I like this is _____________________________________

____.

You should ______________________________________ sometime.

You might like it, too!

Name ______________________________

Read Erica's Paragraph

A Compare Paragraph

Erica wrote a paragraph that tells how milk and water are alike. Read Erica's paragraph.

I think that milk and water are alike in a few ways. You can drink milk and water. Milk does not taste sweet or salty, and water does not taste sweet or salty either. I like to drink both milk and water best when they are cold. I think milk and water are not very different.

Write the topic sentence from Erica's paragraph.

Write one supporting detail sentence from Erica's paragraph.

Write the closing sentence from Erica's paragraph.

Name ______________________________

How They Are the Same

A Compare Paragraph

Write a paragraph that tells
how cats and dogs are alike.
Use Erica's paragraph to help you.

Cats and dogs are alike in several ways. They both

____

____

______________________________.

They also ______________________________

____

____

______________________________.

Finally, ______________________________

____

____

______________________________.

Name ____________________

Read Raffi's Paragraph

A Contrast Paragraph

Raffi wrote a paragraph that tells how video games and board games are different. Read Raffi's paragraph.

Video games are different from board games. You need a screen and buttons to play a video game. To play a board game, you only need the pieces that come with the game. Video games look like cartoons, and board games look like drawings and words in a book. Most video games make sounds, and most board games don't. I like both video games and board games, but they are different.

Write the topic sentence from Raffi's paragraph.

Write one supporting detail sentence from Raffi's paragraph.

Write the closing sentence from Raffi's paragraph.

Name ________________________________

How They Are Different

A Contrast Paragraph

Write a paragraph that tells how ducks and cows are different. Use Raffi's paragraph to help you.

I will write about ____________________ and ____________________.

first thing second thing

How are they different?

____

____

____

Topic Sentence:

____

My Paragraph:

____

____

____

____

Name ______________________

Read Briana's Paragraph

A Narrative Paragraph

Briana wrote a paragraph that tells a story about something that happened to her. Read Briana's paragraph.

I got stung by a jellyfish at the beach. I was swimming in the water, and there was a jellyfish next to me! I touched it by mistake. It stung me, and my arm hurt right away. I felt better later, but I do not want to swim next to a jellyfish ever again!

Write the topic sentence from Briana's paragraph.

Write one supporting detail sentence from Briana's paragraph.

Write the closing sentence from Briana's paragraph.

Name ______________________________

Something That Happened to You

A Narrative Paragraph

Write a paragraph about something that happened to you. Use Briana's paragraph to help you.

Let me tell you about what happened to me. It all started when ______________________________
____
____
______________________________.

Then ______________________________
____
____
______________________________.

I ______________________________
______________________________.

And that is the story of what happened.

Name ____________________

Read Tanya's Paragraph

A Descriptive Paragraph

Tanya wrote a paragraph that tells about her aunt. Read Tanya's paragraph.

Aunt Nina likes to help animals and people. She finds homes for animals. She helps her neighbors grow vegetables in their gardens. She helps me with my math homework. I hope that I will be as kind and helpful as Aunt Nina when I grow up.

Write the topic sentence from Tanya's paragraph.

Write one supporting detail sentence from Tanya's paragraph.

Write the closing sentence from Tanya's paragraph.

Name ______________________________

Someone You Like

A Descriptive Paragraph

Write a paragraph about a person you know and like.
Use Tanya's paragraph to help you.

______________________________ is a person who

I think is ______________________________.

____

____

______________________________.

Another reason is ______________________________

____

____

______________________________.

Also ______________________________.

I like ______________________________ because

______________________________.

Name ______________________

Read Trevor's Paragraph

A How-to Paragraph

Trevor wrote a paragraph that tells how to make nachos. Read Trevor's paragraph.

It is easy to make nachos as a snack. First, I put corn chips on a plate. Then, I put shredded cheese on top of all the chips. Last, I ask my mom to help me melt the cheese on the chips. I like to make nachos because the steps are easy.

Write the topic sentence from Trevor's paragraph.

Write one supporting detail sentence from Trevor's paragraph.

Write the closing sentence from Trevor's paragraph.

Name ______________________________

How to Make It

A How-to Paragraph

Write a paragraph that tells about how to make something that you like to eat. Use Trevor's paragraph to help you.

This is how I make ______________________________

____.

First, I ______________________________________

____.

Then, I ______________________________________

____.

Last, I ______________________________________

____.

This is my favorite way to make ________________

____.

Name ______________________________

Summer Fun!

A Descriptive Paragraph

Write a paragraph that tells about the fun things you like to do in the summer.

There are lots of things I like to do in the summer.

____

____

____

____

____

____

____

____

____

____

____

There is so much we can do during summer.

Name ______________________________

If You Could Be Any Animal

An Opinion Paragraph

Write a paragraph that tells what animal you would be and why.

Being ______________________________ would be terrific!

One reason is that ______________________________

______________________________.

Another reason is ______________________________

______________________________.

Finally, ______________________________

______________________________.

If I were an animal, I would want to be ____________

______________________________.

Name ____________________

Write What You Think

An Opinion Paragraph

Do you think that school recess should be longer or shorter?
Write a paragraph that tells what you think.

I think that school recess ____________________

____________________.

One reason is that ____________________

____________________.

Another reason is ____________________

____________________.

Finally, ____________________

____________________.

This is why I think ____________________.

Name ______________________________

A Time When You Were Scared!

A Narrative Paragraph

Write a paragraph that tells about a time when you were scared.

I felt scared when ______________________________

______________________________.

At first, ______________________________

______________________________.

Then, ______________________________

______________________________.

After, ______________________________

______________________________.

This was one of the times I felt scared.

Name ____________________

A Real Hero

Write a paragraph that tells about a person you think is a hero because he or she helps other people or does good things.

I think ____________________ is a real hero.

This person is a hero because ____________________

____________________.

Also, ____________________

____________________.

Another reason is ____________________

____________________.

These are reasons why ____________________

____________________.

Name ___________________________

If You Had Three Wishes

Write a paragraph that tells what you would wish for if you could have three wishes comes true.

This is what I would wish for if I had three wishes!

The first thing I would wish for ___________________________

___________________________.

Second, I would wish for ___________________________

___________________________.

My third wish would be ___________________________

___________________________.

If these wishes came true, ___________________________

___________________________.

Name ____________________

Write What You Think

If you could eat only one food for the rest of your life, what would it be? Write a paragraph that tells what you think. For your supporting details, tell your reasons for what you think.

Topic Sentence:

____

____

Supporting Detail 1:

____

____

Supporting Detail 2:

____

____

Supporting Detail 3:

____

____

Closing Sentence:

____

____

Answer Key

Page 13
[top left] yes
[top right] no
[center left] no
[center right] yes
[bottom left] yes
[bottom right] no

Page 14
[top left] no
[top right] yes
[bottom left] no
[bottom right] yes
Remaining answer will vary.

Page 15
1. ?
2. ?
3. . or !
4. . or !
5. ?
6. . or !
Remaining answers will vary.

Page 16
1. The girl puts on her socks.
2. Can Amar put on his socks?
3. Our puppy chews on socks.
4. Did you put on your socks?
5. Where are my socks?
(Exclamation points are also acceptable for sentences with periods.)

Page 17
Answers will vary.

Page 18
Answers will vary.

Page 19
Answers will vary.

Page 21
1. thing
2. person
3. place
4. animal
5. person

Page 22
1. Mason
2. A butterfly
3. The swings
4. Eddie
5. The playground
6. A deer
Remaining answer will vary.

Page 23
Answers will vary.

Page 24
1. wears
2. fixes
3. bakes
4. feeds
5. paints
6. rest
7. rakes
8. eats
9. fly

Page 25
1. sniffs the air
2. take their dogs to the park
3. is red
4. has a new puppy
5. feels so soft
6. pets a lot of dogs
Remaining answer will vary.

Page 26
1. predicate
2. subject
3. subject
4. predicate
Remaining answer will vary.

Page 27
Answers will vary.

Page 28
Answers will vary.

Page 30
[top left] linking
[top right] linking
[center left] action
[center right] action
[bottom left] linking
[bottom right] action

Page 31
1. swim; answers will vary
2. jumps; answers will vary
Remaining answers will vary.

Page 32
1. is; answers will vary
2. are; answers will vary
Remaining answers will vary.

Page 33
1. is
2. felt
3. seems
4. are
Remaining answer will vary.

Page 37
Answers will vary.

Page 38
Answers will vary.

Page 39
Answers will vary.

Page 40
Answers will vary.

Page 41
Answers will vary.

Page 42
Answers will vary.

Page 43
Answers will vary.

Page 44
Answers will vary.

Page 45
Answers will vary.

Page 47
how
when
how
where
how

Page 48
Answers will vary.

Page 49
Answers will vary.

Page 51
Answers will vary.

Page 52
Answers will vary.

Page 53
Answers will vary.

Page 54
Answers will vary.

Page 55
Answers will vary.

Page 56
Answers will vary.

Page 57
Answers will vary.

Page 58
Answers will vary.

Page 59
Answers will vary.

Page 63
no
yes
no
yes

Page 64
yes
no
yes

Page 65
yes
no
yes

Page 67
Sometimes I wish that I could fly.

Meena learned how to ride a bike.

Mike's favorite food is soup.

Alicia's family gave some of their things to a place that helps people.

Page 68

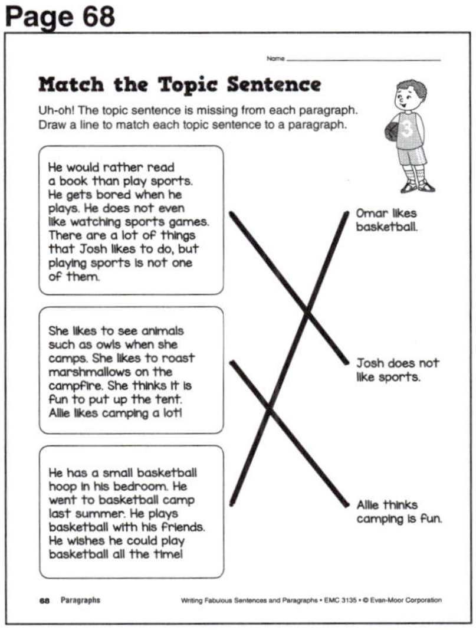
Name

Match the Topic Sentence

Uh-oh! The topic sentence is missing from each paragraph. Draw a line to match each topic sentence to a paragraph.

He would rather read a book than play sports. He gets bored when he plays. He does not even like watching sports games. There are a lot of things that Josh likes to do, but playing sports is not one of them.

She likes to see animals such as owls when she camps. She likes to roast marshmallows on the campfire. She thinks it is fun to put up the tent. Allie likes camping a lot!

He has a small basketball hoop in his bedroom. He went to basketball camp last summer. He plays basketball with his friends. He wishes he could play basketball all the time!

Omar likes basketball.

Josh does not like sports.

Allie thinks camping is fun.

68 Paragraphs   Writing Fabulous Sentences and Paragraphs • EMC 3135 • © Evan-Moor Corporation

Page 69
Shanice ordered a pizza.
Craig takes good care of his dog.
Britney and Selena are alike.

Page 70
(Answers will vary. Examples shown.)
Dogs can eat
when I feel cold
milkshake flavors

Page 71
Families can be different.

People can choose how they want to play music.

Page 72
First, he puts away his backpack and shoes. Second, he sweeps the kitchen floor. Third, he helps his dad cook dinner.

Baby frogs are called tadpoles.
Baby cows are called calves.
Baby kangaroos are called joeys.

Ashley likes baseball best, and Dana likes hockey best. Ashley likes to wear jeans, and Dana likes to wear leggings. Ashley likes pasta, but Dana does not like pasta at all.

Page 73
They are quiet.

It is fun to watch them swim.

They are neat pets that do not make a mess in your house.

Page 74
She looks for numbers everywhere she goes.

She likes to add numbers together to find a sum.

Jill also likes to do subtraction.

Page 75
He tells funny jokes.
Koalas have big round eyes.

Page 76
Answers will vary.

Page 77
Some people think mice are cute.

Sometimes you can find bird nests in trees.

A lot of people like to eat candy when they watch a movie.

Page 78
Some people work as firefighters.

Third, he lays his full uniform out on his dresser.

Page 79
Answers will vary.

Page 80
Pearl would wear her favorite shirt every day if she could!

Hank exercises every day.

Ava told her parents that she would do anything for a pet fox.

Salads are one of the family's favorite foods to make.

Page 81

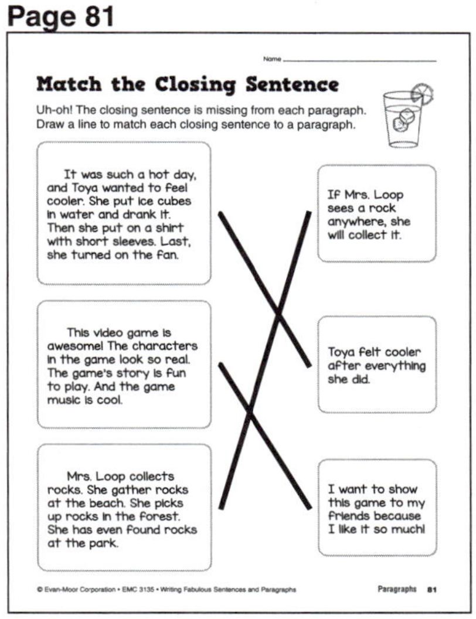
Name

Match the Closing Sentence

Uh-oh! The closing sentence is missing from each paragraph. Draw a line to match each closing sentence to a paragraph.

It was such a hot day, and Toya wanted to feel cooler. She put ice cubes in water and drank it. Then she put on a shirt with short sleeves. Last, she turned on the fan.

This video game is awesome! The characters in the game look so real. The game's story is fun to play. And the game music is cool.

Mrs. Loop collects rocks. She gather rocks at the beach. She picks up rocks in the forest. She has even found rocks at the park.

If Mrs. Loop sees a rock anywhere, she will collect it.

Toya felt cooler after everything she did.

I want to show this game to my friends because I like it so much!

© Evan-Moor Corporation • EMC 3135 • Writing Fabulous Sentences and Paragraphs   Paragraphs 81

Page 82
These are just a few ways that cars and bikes are alike.

Max is a really great dog.

Page 83
(Answers will vary. Examples shown.)
are the same
I am excited
Think of ways

Page 84
make a smoothie with almost any foods

Many people recycle

Page 85
Answers will vary.

Page 86
Answers will vary.

Page 87
Answers will vary.

Page 91
I like comic books.

Answers will vary but must be one of the three middle sentences from the paragraph.

I like comic books because they are fun to read.

Page 92
Answers will vary.

Page 93
I think that milk and water are alike in a few ways.

Answers will vary but must be one of the three middle sentences from the paragraph.

I think milk and water are not very different.

Page 94
Answers will vary.

Page 95
Video games are different from board games.

Answers will vary but must be one of the three middle sentences from the paragraph.

I like both video games and board games, but they are different.

Page 96
Answers will vary.

Page 97
I got stung by a jellyfish at the beach.

Answers will vary but must be one of the three middle sentences from the paragraph.

I felt better later, but I do not want to swim next to a jellyfish ever again!

Page 98
Answers will vary.

Page 99
Aunt Nina likes to help animals and people.

Answers will vary but must be one of the three middle sentences from the paragraph.

I hope that I will be as kind and helpful as Aunt Nina when I grow up.

Page 100
Answers will vary.

Page 101
It is easy to make nachos as a snack.

Answers will vary but must be one of the three middle sentences from the paragraph.

I like to make nachos because the steps are easy.

Page 102
Answers will vary.

Page 103
Answers will vary.

Page 104
Answers will vary.

Page 105
Answers will vary.

Page 106
Answers will vary.

Page 107
Answers will vary.

Page 108
Answers will vary.

Page 109
Answers will vary.